African-American Heroes

Denzel Washington

Stephen Feinstein

Enslow Elementary
an imprint of

 Enslow Publishers, Inc.
40 Industrial Road
Box 398
Berkeley Heights, NJ 07922
USA

http://www.enslow.com

Words to Know

agent—A person who finds parts in movies and plays for people.

boarding school—A school at which students live.

counselor (COWN-suh-ler)—A person who looks after kids at a summer camp.

spokesman—Someone who speaks for a company or group.

strict—Having strong rules that must be followed.

Enslow Elementary, an imprint of Enslow Publishers, Inc.

Enslow Elementary® is a registered trademark of Enslow Publishers, Inc.

Library of Congress Cataloging-in-Publication Data

Feinstein, Stephen.

    Denzel Washington / Stephen Feinstein.

        p. cm. — (African-American heroes)

    Includes index.

    Summary: "Elementary biography of actor Denzel Washington discussing his childhood, his struggle and triumph as an actor, and how he gives back to the community"—Provided by publisher.

    ISBN-13: 978-0-7660-2895-1

    ISBN-10: 0-7660-2895-X

    1. Washington, Denzel, 1954–   —Juvenile literature.

2. Actors—United States—Biography—Juvenile literature.

3. African American actors—Biography—Juvenile literature.

I. Title.

    PN2287.W452F45 2009

    791.4302'8092—dc22

    [B]

                       2007038447

Printed in the United States of America

10 9 8 7 6 5 4 3 2

To Our Readers: We have done our best to make sure all Internet Addresses in this book were active and appropriate when we went to press. However, the author and the publisher have no control over and assume no liability for the material available on those Internet sites or on links to other Web sites. Any comments or suggestions can be sent by e-mail to comments@enslow.com or to the address on the back cover.

♻ Enslow Publishers, Inc., is committed to printing our books on recycled paper. The paper in every book contains 10% to 30% post-consumer waste (PCW). The cover board on the outside of each book contains 100% PCW. Our goal is to do our part to help young people and the environment too!

Illustration Credits: AP/Wide World, pp. 1, 2, 3, 5, 13, 16 (left), 19, 21, back cover; courtesy Boys & Girls Clubs of America, pp. 3, 7, 20; Everett Collection, pp. 3, 14, 16 (right), 17, 18; Melissa Segal, pp. 10–11; Getty Images, p. 15; Shutterstock, p. 9.

Cover Illustration: AP/Wide World.

Contents

Chapter 1

Growing Up in Mount Vernon

Denzel Washington was born on December 28, 1954, in Mount Vernon, New York. He was named after his father, who was a minister. Denzel's mother, Lennis, worked in a beauty parlor.

Denzel's parents were very **strict**. They expected the best of Denzel, his older sister, Lorice, and his younger brother, David. Denzel's father did not let the children see movies, except for films about religion. So Denzel was not a big fan of movies at that time.

Denzel Washington grew up to become one of America's best movie actors.

Denzel was a happy child. He had many friends. Some of them were African American. Some were from the West Indies. Denzel also had Italian and Irish friends. He learned a lot about many different kinds of people.

When Denzel was six, he joined the Mount Vernon Boys Club. There he learned to play football and basketball. Denzel was popular because he was good at sports. Later, he said, "In my neighborhood the Boys Club was the center of everything. It was my whole world, just about, from the time I was six years old."

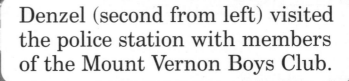

Denzel (second from left) visited the police station with members of the Mount Vernon Boys Club.

Denzel (circled in green) played on the Boys Club football team.

Chapter 2 Hard Times

When Denzel was fourteen, his happy world changed. His parents' marriage ended. Denzel's father moved far away to Virginia. Now Lennis had to raise her three children all by herself.

Denzel could not understand why his parents separated. He was mad. He got into fights with other kids. He hung out with boys who were always getting into trouble. Some of them later ended up in prison.

Denzel's mother did not want him hanging out with a bad crowd. She sent him away to a private **boarding school** for boys. Denzel lived at the school. He came home only on holidays.

Denzel did not study hard at school. He was more interested in sports than anything else. He played baseball, basketball, and football. But when Denzel graduated, his grades were good enough for him to go to college.

Denzel liked to play sports, just like these students.

In 1972, Denzel went to Fordham University in New York City. His first plan was to study to become a doctor. But the science classes were too hard for him. Soon he fell far behind. His grades were very poor.

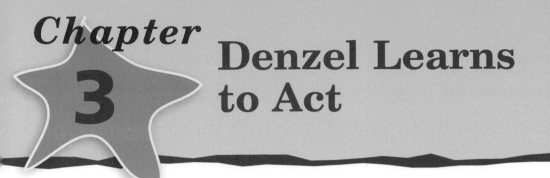

Fordham University in New York City. Denzel found the science classes there very hard.

The next year, Denzel left Fordham. He worked at the post office. Then he got a job collecting garbage. He was not happy at his jobs. So Denzel decided to go back to college. But he did not know what to study.

That summer, Denzel got a job as a **counselor** at a YMCA camp. He and the other counselors put on a play for the kids. While acting in the play, Denzel liked being on the stage. Suddenly he saw a new path for his life.

Denzel went back to Fordham. One of his classes was acting. The teacher, Robinson Stone, was an actor. He taught Denzel all about acting on the stage.

The next year, Denzel acted in a play called *The Emperor Jones* at Fordham. Denzel liked learning his lines. He liked being out in front of people. Denzel now knew for sure what he wanted to do with his life.

Denzel Becomes a Big Star

During his last year at Fordham, Denzel acted in *Othello*, a famous play by William Shakespeare. The audience loved him. Robinson Stone knew an **agent**, someone who finds parts in movies and plays for people. He brought the agent to see Denzel in the play. The agent got Denzel a part in the TV movie *Wilma*. His first day on the set, Denzel met Pauletta Pearson, a young woman who sang in Broadway shows. Denzel and Pauletta soon fell in love.

Denzel met Pauletta Pearson while making a TV movie.

Denzel graduated from college in 1977. For several years he kept trying to get parts in shows and movies. It was very hard because there were many good actors also trying for the same parts. But Denzel never gave up.

In 1981, Denzel won several awards for acting in plays. The next year he began his part as Dr. Phillip Chandler in the TV series *St. Elsewhere*.

Denzel played a doctor in the TV show *St. Elsewhere*.

In 1983, Denzel married Pauletta.
Later they had four children: John David,
Katia, and twins Malcolm and Olivia.

Denzel and Pauletta have four
children. Here they are with some
other family members. Denzel's
mother is standing in front of him.

Denzel with his sons, John
David (on left) and Malcolm,
in 1999.

Denzel began to get leading parts in movies. He won awards for his acting in *Glory*. This was a movie about African-American soldiers who fought for the North in the American Civil War.

In *Glory*, Denzel played a Union soldier.

Denzel (center) as a soldier in *Glory*, with Jihmi Kennedy (left) and Morgan Freeman (right).

In 1992, Denzel played the title role in the movie *Malcolm X*. He was a famous leader who fought for freedom for African Americans.

In *Malcolm X*, Denzel played a famous African-American leader.

Denzel's acting brought him millions of fans. By 1998, he was one of the country's top ten most popular movie stars. In 2002, Denzel got an Academy Award for Best Actor for the movie *Training Day*.

Here is Denzel with Halle Berry, who won the Best Actress award.

Denzel speaks out for the Boys &
Girls Clubs of America because he
wants to help young people.

Denzel became a **spokesman** for the
Boys & Girls Clubs of America, because
he had been a member of the Boys Club in
Mount Vernon. He said the club was very
important to him, and he wanted other
kids to get a chance to be in the club too.

Once Denzel knew that he wanted to be an actor, he worked hard to make it happen. Denzel tells young people that they can also make their hopes and dreams come true.

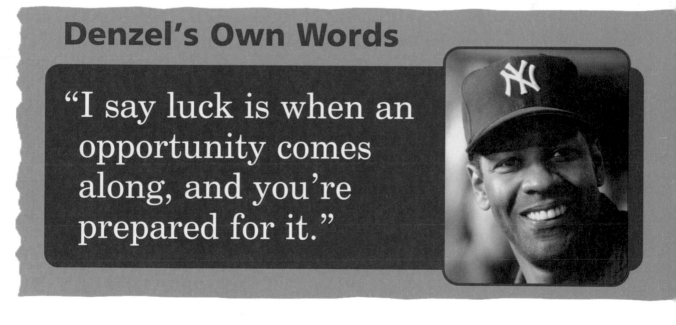

Denzel's Own Words

"I say luck is when an opportunity comes along, and you're prepared for it."

Timeline

1954—Denzel is born in Mount Vernon, New York, on December 28.

1960—Denzel joins the Mount Vernon Boys Club.

1968—Denzel's parents separate. Denzel goes to a private boarding school.

1972—Denzel begins studying at Fordham University in New York City.

1977—Denzel graduates from Fordham University.

1982—Denzel begins to play Dr. Phillip Chandler in the TV series *St. Elsewhere*.

1983—Denzel and Pauletta Pearson get married.

1989—Denzel wins an award for acting in the movie *Glory*.

1992—Denzel wins an award for acting in the movie *Malcolm X*. He becomes national spokesman for Boys & Girls Club of America.

2002—Denzel receives an Academy Award for Best Actor for his part in *Training Day*.

Learn More

Books

Bany-Winters, Lisa. *On Stage: Theater Games and Activities for Kids*. Chicago: Chicago Review Press, 1997.

Wheeler, Jill C. *Denzel Washington*. Minneapolis: ABDO, 2003.

Wilson, Mike. *Denzel Washington*. London: Hodder and Stoughton, 2003.

Web Sites

Boys & Girls Clubs of America
<http://www.bgca.org>

Denzel Washington Biography
<http://www.biography.com>
   Go to "Search," type in "Denzel Washington," then click on "Washington, Denzel."

Index